Every Slow Thing

Every Slow Thing

Poems by

Daniel Lusk

Cover design by Shay Culligan
Cover art by Adelaide Murphy Tyrol,
Map of the World (Ingres)
Author photo by Alison Redlich

ISBN: 978-1-63980-119-0

Kelsay Books
502 South 1040 East, A-119
American Fork, Utah 84003
Kelsaybooks.com

For Angela

Acknowledgments

Poems in this collection first appeared in the following journals:

Barrow Street Review: "Paleo Truleo"

Cloudbank: "There is a Saying in Swahili"

Crosswinds Poetry Journal: "Ah, Now," "Before"

Cutbank: "Circus"

Gulf Coast: "Dakota 1969"

Hawaii Pacific Review: "Signs of Spring"

Innisfree Poetry Journal: "Anthropology,"
    "As Beauty Does," "Nocturne No. 2 in E Flat Major,"
    "Poet, Old School"

Live Encounters: "Asp of Jerusalem," "Dawn at Seapoint,"
    "Glencolmcille," "In My Hometown," "Kiss the Lion,"
    "Morning Inchigeelah," "Nine Green Apples,"
    "Nude in a Cathedral Window," "Omenclature,"
    "On Goose Pond," "Pastoral"

Massachusetts Review: "Legacy"

New Letters: "At the Baptist Church," "The Hermit
    Speaks to His Dogs"

Nimrod International Journal: "Bane," "Deeds,"

    "How the Story Begins: *Prelude to a Ballet,*"

    "Robyn of the Snows," "The Oat Witch and the Old

    Man's Daughters," "Storm" (as "When Horses Love"),

    "Veterans Day," "Weights and Measures"

North American Review: "Water Music," "Reverie"

Off the Coast: "For My Wife on Her Birthday,"

    "On the Death of a Small Child," "Old Man Feet"

Prairie Schooner: "Pentimento"

Salamander: "The Palmist"

Spillway: "Night-walking"

Stonecoast Review: "Olly Olly Oxen Free"

The Café Review: "Things to Say Underwater"

The Chariton Review: "Triptych" (as "Midwest Memoir")

The South Dakota Review: "Haystacks Like Bread"

The Tahoma Review: "Self-portrait with Cat"

Contents

Every Slow Thing

The life so short, the craft so long to lerne.
Geoffrey Chaucer

Glencolmcille

—County Donegal, Ireland

The cliffs here
refuse the sea,
over and over

and over. Yet
see this rockfall—

once
in a thousand years,
they yield.

Preludes

Signs of Spring

For some, it's a robin.
For him, a spider in the sink.

A yellow birch down
across the lane, white slush
a hand's breadth deep,
floating on the mud.

These holes in the ground,
these smallest of caves,
dwellings of the meek: voles,
yellow-spotted salamanders.

The rewards of raking appear
because our heads are bowed.

A patch of blue sky
opens in the clouds,
warm wind in urgent gusts.

Across the woods, beginning
on the tips of a maple tree
by the pond, a single red filament
appears like a wound.

Somewhere nearby
the she-bear lifts her head.

On Goose Pond

—after a photograph by Carolyn Bates

What bird is singing on Goose Pond
this early day of cricket din
and tree frog choir?

Now and again goose-in-residence
will snore, breaking her fast
and maybe then what troubles a distant loon
to sing the blues it seems.

This red, not blood on the water but
a bruised reflection of some far-off wound;
that's the way it would appear—
anger heart-sore fire-in-a-bottle blown.

And, here, sweet peace for us, the mirror
of whatever blow has creased
the fabric of our brother world
a shimmering silence. Now and again a bird.

These murmurs on our ear
of cricket, frog, and goose
mere fractals of soul-shattering sounds
we might catch wind of late
tomorrow, loves. Be safe. Be kind.

Dawn at Seapoint

First the blue water, pale
and reverential. Seen from a broad window
above the rooftops, past the dog-blind
skylights of shadow buildings
off Belgrave Square.

Now pearl grey-and-sandglass sea.
Almost spirit approaching imperceptibly,
cleaving to the far edge of horizon
whence it comes.

A winking buoy warning no one
echoed by glimmering lights of Howth
beyond and shadow mountains of Wales
farther on across the way.

A single bird pedals over the soldiering
silhouettes of stoic chimney pots.
The baleful cry of a black-backed gull
harks to the frail quality of mercy
that envelops the sleeping town.

Glow of a streetlight off a tall hedge
by the seafront. No cyclist on the road,
no dog-walker, no swimmer with rolled togs
under her arm returning home.

A blackbird pipes from a garden wall.
Wood pigeon and taxi man,
like my father born this day in June, yet asleep.

How the Story Begins: Prelude to a Ballet

A girl steps out of the trees.

What she is wearing,
her first gesture upon emerging
from those woods—these will matter
little to the story.

If she takes off her shoe,
or bends from the waist to tighten the laces.
If she adjusts her clothes—the loose
chambray shirt, or the snug cardigan.
Maybe she smooths the seat of her trousers.

If she looks up at the sun
or at the moon.
Or shields her eyes with one hand.

Whether she glances furtively
over her shoulder
toward the woods behind her
as if she heard something—a twig snap
or a strange, almost human bird call.

If she appears to notice
that her shirt is buttoned unevenly,
and begins to redo it,
first one button, then the next.

Suppose she begins at the bottom
to correct the mistake, each step
requiring she first unbutton
the previous, errant fastening, and so on.
As if she were learning the clarinet.

If she finds at the last step her garment
is even more askew
and begins again, this time with the button
at her chest, where
she was bitten by a mosquito.

It would be simpler, better,
we imagine from our distant
perspective, if she simply
undid the garment altogether
to begin again.

Perhaps she removes a bottle
from her backpack and drinks long.
Wipes her hands absently
on her clothes.

If she twirls a leaf between her fingers,
or places it between her thumbs
and puts it to her lips.
Or lifts the wild blossom
she carries to her face.

If she begins to run begins
to walk quickly aimlessly
looks side to side, or far ahead,
looks at the ground.

Maybe a bird flies past overhead,
a gold thread in its beak. Or
the shadow of a bird with a strand
of hair. Or no bird but the shadow
of a cloud, scudding across the grass,
across her face.

If she stands still and stretches
her slender arms high over her head.
If she bends deeply from the waist,
her shirt riding open to reveal a tattoo,
her long legs partly obscured.
Fingers appearing to touch the earth.

Watching her, I believe
a hair from the head
of a comely stranger, or a pale stain
from a cheap ankle bracelet,
can change the rules of nature.

She may forget what she saw earlier
from hiding, through the limbs
of witch hazel, there among ferns,
on the bright green moss
beside the rotting tree.

She may remember forever
the two of them locked together,
her surprise, their fur,
their wild bird flutter,
her heart's clamor, their animal voices.

She may take off her other shoe
and continue, barefooted,
across the broad and undulating field.

May sense someone watching
as she advances, dancing inside
to some private music,
a little spring at the knees.

Perhaps her arms are extended
generously, palms up, to show
how she might surrender.
How she might carry a newborn.
Might carry the dead.

Morning Inchigeelagh

—for J.F. (1937–2016)

The roof has come off the church
and rain is falling in the baptistry.
The metaphorical sheep of the Testament
graze the green sanctuary
and swallows whisper over the grass.

Across the way a vault of sycamores
behind a scrim of hurried lace, garment
of one who will not come out
from under the stone.

And look! The sudden sunshine
where we walked among roses and aquilegia.
Butterflies and lilies, too,
languid on the frog pond. A hymn
to summer everlasting.

Anon, I will take my turn at the garden gate,
holding the white end of the golden thread.

But now, too long away to weep,
to grieve my friend,
I watch the rain, the baptistry, the holy sheep.
And do what I have been given to do.

Water Music

All night
a slow, filigree rain.

Enter the dreamer
barefoot as a child,
in a birch-bark tuxedo.

Frogs in the footlights.
Bears in the balcony.

Clouds play Haydn
as they cross the moon.

He dreams the pond
is a blue piano.

Morning in Glasthule

I wake to the bin men
bashing the bins.

Lights on in clerestory windows
of the Harold School.
Sun on the slates.

A fine day so far.
Only a rag of cloud.

Magpies lording over the gardens.
Sparrows playing
odds and evens on the wires.

New Year's Poem

The purpose of dreams—
to remind us which foot goes forward
when we leap over fences
and burning barricades. To warn us

that upon waking
we are no longer nimble.

Today I'll stop pretending
that I get to stay home and drink tea
while others get dressed
and go to their jobs.

Perhaps the coyote will come
for the last turkey hen and no one
will notice.

Condors and their cousins exchange
secret messages when they pass
on the stairs. The meaning
is in the red sealing wax on the envelopes.

Vermeer made sure that the pitcher
in the painting would never be empty
and the bowl would never overflow.

My blood pressure is rising.
I appear to be slowing down. But
I'm approaching the speed of light.

No Song But Breathing

"...there are some accounts that can't be settled."
Wendell Berry, *Jayber Crow*

Triptych

1. Theotany: Night Harvester

Once we were carnivores
like the cats and crows,
and then we discovered corn.

This is North Iowa.
Night is a field, a luminous cloud.
Its grumbling, furious god
glowers from a shroud
of pollen and dust.

Beyond our car lights
grain elevators rise
like steeples in the halo
of the town-lit horizon.

Believers swear the giant eats
the choicest grains,
to turn them into stars.

In a generous year
when the forests of tassels
are churned into silage,
and ears like bearded wallets
are shelled into country shekels,

cribs and sheds and storage bins
overflow onto broad streets
of towns like a magpie's paradise,
mountains of gold.

Some thank heaven
and wish their dead could fly.
I am one who trusts
the implacable wind.

2. *Bounty*

When the slatted cribs bulged,
and the round metal bins
in the fields, the towering
grain elevators overflowed,

they piled shelled corn
in the broad street of town

until it rose
in shining dunes,
higher than our houses.

Gold nobody wanted
made them poor,
and only the pigs grew fat.

3. *Kin*

Farmers never stopped telling
of the year the crickets came.

Hard to think them your sisters
when they crawl over each other
in your shoes at the back of the closet,

or your brothers,
in the pockets of your Sunday suit.

Hens had a field day,
snatching them off toys in the sandbox,
off the steps to the back stoop.

They swam in the cooking pots
soaking in the sink.
Rummaged the everyday silver
in the drawer, next to plates at the table.

Then, as by a signal,
some breath of wind over the Indian Ocean,
some shrug of a distant glacier, gone.

In My Hometown

She sits on the curbstone,
picking a scab on her knee.

The boys are watching haircuts
through the window of the barber's
caravan and pay her no mind.

At the corner Rexall store teens
sit on the steps out front, sipping fizzy
cream sodas and cherry cokes.

Now and again a matronly Buick
or austere Lincoln Continental ghosts by
like a premonition of time to come.

Coach says we are better
now the season is over. If only.

In the sound booth at the record store
Chet Baker plays "Every Time
We Say Goodbye." After the last plaint
of the boozy trumpet, a little rift of silence…

like the purple aura of our mother's arms
as she tells us about a prayer circle
around a neighbor's sickbed.

In my hometown, life in a minor key.

After the War

Not the moon, but the idea of the moon,
its tidal power moving nothing he can see.

Nothing so plain as a field of corn
in midday heat, hemmed by redundant
barbed-wire fences, as though a rogue stalk
might attempt escape, might bolt
from the battalion of tender swords,
chafing at each sodden gust.

And here humidity distills the night air
to a heady liqueur, tangible in the mouth as water.

Brow of his house thrust out among
the broad, leafy shroud of an ancient sycamore.
High up in a bedroom window
he lies almost naked on the bedsheets, elbows
on the sill, forehead against the screen.
He might be Zacchaeus, too small to see over
the crowd, straining to catch a word,
to catch at any moving breath at all.

Behind him, soft percussion of brother's
rhythmic breathing. Too warm to hum the tune.

This is the church of night—call and response
of serenading crickets. Scritch of cricket one
and cricket two. Hoo-hoo of a mothering owl
mocks his blindness from her airy sanctuary.

Now and again out of the greater dark
a shout of warning or a curse. Not,
he guesses, the veteran amputee outside
the house next door, smoking in the dark,
listening to the peace he won.

No one so solitary as a soldier
made redundant by the loss of limbs,
seated in a coaster wagon on the sidewalk
by his porch, waiting for tomorrow
and the mail in its secret manila envelope.

Flakes of laughter as visitors leave the doorstep
of the twin girls down the block.
He'd like to know their secrets. What code
is signaled by the ice company delivery card
in the window on the wrong day.

None so intimate as clusters of grapes
that dandle among the shadows of leaves
beneath the garden hedgerow, nor so inviting
to the tongue as he lay humming yesterday *this
and this and this Amen* within his hiding place.

Strains of Bach minuets unwind from the far end
of the street where his bachelor piano teacher sits
alone at his keyboard. In mind's eye, the last house
before the woods begin, and beyond,
the sleeping cemetery.

Moon no moon.
This is the endless *and, and, and* of August…

Pastoral

Barefoot, wading where the river
laps and eddies, where summer cows
come to drink, a boy

dabbling in shallows
to see what I might see—

a clam, embedded in sand,
itself delving or luxuriating it seemed,

shell excoriated, hard as shale
or horse's hoof, or blind church door.

Did not part to lick its lips, did not sing
to me as I naïve expected
and might have done, am not past doing

at any command now, whisper
at the ear in French *s'il vous plait*, kiss
on the eyelids or behind the knee.

Tried to guess the spell or charm
who could not imagine soul or pearl
or salt viscosity within the stolid lips
of that hard reticule. Who had not art

to evoke or feel the chuckle and moan
of pleasure known since books
were slabs of clay and papyrus rolls

or knew what claim of sanctuary
may keep away the human clamor,
disguise the clap and swerve
of true religion at play inside.

Deeps

It's the child learning to count
eins, zwei, drei...elf, zwölf...

It's the boy aroused by fervent singing
in a candle-lighted church, heart quivering,
soul giddy as a kite in a gale pray for me...

who will negotiate the knees of grown-ups,
throw himself upon the avuncular arms of Jesus.

It's the lads at camp, pretending to be soldiers
in the dark, chest deep in murky water,
or prisoners, arms up to ward off unseen branches,
mosquitoes pray for me who cannot swim

crows call this way call there a young one
tries...elf or zwölf...there may be
wolves about and he a lamb.

The big boys run naked and hell-bent
and he runs shouting after to pitch
headlong upon the outstretched arms
of the muddy river pray for me, pray or swim.

Veterans' Day

Whenever a war is remembered,
old men stand accused.

Their accusers the same
as witnesses in their defense—
a grass bracelet at the back
of an underwear drawer;
a rifle ball brother
to a scar on the cheek;

a captured flag folded in the attic;
this bundle of letters in a woman's hand.
We pray there is no gold tooth
among nails in a hidden coffee can.

I did not kill him, but I ate his portion of rice.

After the gun salute over the grave
my friend plays Taps on his gold cornet
and it lifts on the wind
across adjacent farmland.

Hidden by arborvitae
a generation of gravestones away,
I echo his tune on my dented trumpet
ironic and thin, as if
from stairs of a clapboard purgatory.

What does it mean, he was wearing his brother's coat?

Remember it now,
we marched among
the thousand thousand flags

to clickety-click of drummers' sticks
on the rims, our feet
scuffing the cemetery road in time.

Those muffled feet, remember
that was also us, dead
and going away to a future war;
that was us, silenced and falling,
our mouths filled with our portion of life.

At the Baptist Church

Blind preacher appears in white,
waist deep before the faded mural of a river
behind the baptistry. Lifts his hand
to the mural of heaven in his mind, quotes
beatitudes vaguely scriptural.

Pipe organ moans a quavering note.
Old Zekiel snores, alone in his pew. Starts
and sighs Amen. Prodigal, home
from abroad, wonders—that dusky woman
bent over her hymnal, did she

kiss him when they were fourteen,
hidden among choir robes, odor of mothballs.
Desire—*eau de civet*. Gulls
over the faded river cry out to the drowning.
He vows to learn French.

What did the prophet whisper
to the woman drawing water? he muses.
And what did she reply? Something in Aramaic.

Prodigal, he knows they will say.
Yes, we were there, he will say.
It was Nina Simone on piano,
a blue shadow on the floor behind her

like the puddled heap of a blue dress.

Storm

—for my father

When horses mate, it seems
an immense thing passes—war,
conversion, coming of age, or
a prairie storm—

wind lashing crowns of oaks and maples,
gold and scarlet flags, virgin oats
and rye threshed green in the fields by hail
like shards of glass,
wild pounding of the haymow doors

and watching them stamp and whistle
we might be afraid
but there is too much of wonder.

It is the same in heart-racing weather,
roof beat and mutter of falling water,
runoff in the gutters,
rain larruping the flailing branches.

Blowing in the open window,
lifting the curtains,
sweat-wet on the page where I write.

Thunderstorms were metaphors
for wildness I knew our father felt,
heartache and regret and turmoil inside.

He watched them come, great
towering spinnakers of rampant thunderclouds,
roil, and churn, and billow, a gathering
madness above us over the westward pasture.

The two of us stood, larger
and small, awestruck, apart,
faces canted to the expanding skies.

Think mare and stallion at reckless gallop,
wheeling at the fences,
manes and tails flying, teeth bared
to neck and haunch and withers,
rearing to paw the wind. Screaming!

Sometimes at night,
he stood on the wide porch
or at the open windows, unmoving.
Lightning cleaved the dark.
Thunder rocked the house.

While our mother roused us
from our beds upstairs, hearts hammering,
scrawny-legged in our underwear,
shepherded into dank safety of the coal bin
in the washing cellar,

he stared, transfixed,
and smoke curled outward
from his cigarette as from a lighted fuse.

Sometimes a sound surrounded us,
crowding our chests to hurt,
shutting our throats

as if the thunder spoke,
as if some voice within,
some resonance returned the rumbling
as human song.

I learned never to ask
what made him weep and sing.

Or why life seemed so ordinary otherwise.

Occasions of Concupiscence/Bliss

—for E. and C.G.

Because they slept naked, the train
keening the crossing far down the mile
like wolves, like themselves in their hunger
and sleepless languor on country nights.

Days in the field she walked the stubble
to bring him a cold beer in the shade,
her fingertips wet from the mist on the can
touching the dusted hairs of his arm,
the stubble of his jaw when they kissed.

Because they slept naked, except for hard rain
and thunder, the windows ajar, the engine sobbing
its climb to the trestle, whelming their limbs
like an aural skin, mocking their yes and no.

Intake of their breaths at its sudden cry
splitting the hot space between them,
recalling the dare and the carefree race
to the homeward crossing, the spit and roar.

They would sleep naked, but throbbing music
and the rain kept them to last call at the roadhouse.

Homeward, glad they had danced and drunk
to the moon that moonless night, for lightning
and a daring road. As it happened, their wheels
first scried the crossing, the blinding glare, the train.

Legacy

...sometimes a whistle is all you've got.
Jill Lapore, "In Every Dark Hour" *The New Yorker*

We had reasons to fear the dark.

The stories we were told
not meant to comfort: How lonely
to be inside that whale.
The warm barn smell grown nasty
after weeks on board that ark.

Never mind the woman who gave herself
to an enemy general and in the night
drove a stake through his head—like that.

We believed in a Holy Ghost
so tangible it could knock you down the stairs
with the back of its hand.

I learned to whistle when I was seven
because you never know.

One time the guy who whistled
the theme for the movie "The High and the Mighty"
came for a school assembly
and did that for us—whistled. And

with just a doorknob, a plunger, a microphone
and a pan of gravel, showed how eerie radio sound
effects—creaking doors, clip-clop horses' hooves
and such were made. Sheet metal thunder.
We paid attention. You never know.

Night also has reasons to listen up.
Its languages: tree frogs, crickets, owls.
Screams of cats. We lock our windows,
doors, sleep with a light, try not to dream.

The Oat Witch & the Old Man's Daughters

It's an old story
and I suffered it.
How the patriarch fell
and the tractor fell silent.

How wind stirred
among the crowd of oat sheaves
left standing in the field

as if his spirit
waited among them.

How a stranger came
in the guise of a preacher
to lift, unwitting, the last
sheaf to the wagon.

Who bent his head to the load
in prayer or resignation.

How the sheaf-goat
dressed as a child
lifted a pitchfork to stick it
into the wagonload
as the tractor lept ahead.

How the stranger,
as in a ritual of harvest,
came to be killed.

I was that stranger. I
bled to the tines'
victorious singing. Bled
for the Oat Witch's hunger.

They laid me down
by the howling thresher,
torn half-naked
and shorn of disguise.

Cleansed and poulticed
my body with unguents
so I no longer knew myself
or how long I died

but awoke one day to silence
and the curious balm
conferred on my wounds
by the old man's daughters.

Haystacks Like Bread

Years later, the haystacks
I learned to build
with a tractor and hydraulic fork
had shrunk to crusty lumps

like a village of thatched hovels
among the ragged stalks
of fireweed and hollyhocks
by the corral fence

no eyes, no brain, no beating heart
—and yet were still alive.

Snakes, mice, dung beetles, ticks,
mites, bacteria and mold
inside the dried and faded hides
yes and pungent hay—
green alfalfa, yellowed timothy,
red clover stems and flowers faded blue.

Gathered after the mower
and the rake onto long steel fingers
of the ample apron on the old John Deere,
lifted high and laid in the tangled, yeasty
cross-hatch of one another's arms

they rose like bread dough
into compact architecture like houses,
stables, barns. They were my churches.
Loaves and fishes for cattle gathered
at the long white tables of frigid winter.

Not spent, in time become field museums
for the shadow of the red-tailed hawk
skating over the creek bottom,
for funereal buzzards, come
to pace their stubble dooryards,
alert to reek of dead field mouse,
rattlesnake, brooding prairie hen
or cottontail eviscerated by the twenty knives
of the mower's clattering arm.

Museums too for the whine
of mosquitoes, noxious clouds
of fireweed pollen, echoes
of prairie dog whistle, hornet's fizz and sting

for drooze of soon-to-be-calving cows,
lather of the neighbor's daughter's horse
at pounding gallop,
for cackle of a solitary cottonwood
in the calculating wind

for bull spunk and coyote's jawbone,
antelope skull, smoke of fur and flesh
off a steer calf bawling under a branding iron.

Chambered and shuttered concert halls
of songs I howled over the tractor's roar
as I gathered stem, strand and flower
to lift and lave and invest with my own
jubilant curses, wild promises, regrets
and misremembered names.

Pentimento

When the bull
comes out of the truck,
he does not ask permission
of the keeper with his limp
drover's whip.

For a young man numbed
by rules, the admonitions
of an impotent father,
this is a sign.

He sees the bull is his mentor.

If the bull explodes,
hooves and pizzle
and hammering balls,

and shatters the gate,

the apprentice will also leap,
vaulting the barrier chute,
torn flesh of his ribs
the price of escape.

Maybe,
even as he falls in a cloud
of pollen, his descent
embraced by a crowd of fireweed,
he will begin to rise.   .

Blood and abrasions no badge
of humility, yet marks of a lesson
only the bull could teach him.

56

Deeds

No song but breathing,
and no heat but bodies:
of this cow where she lies
steaming in cold window light,

of this hired hand who gathers
stout rope to secure her for the work,
of this tall man, worn satchel at his feet.

They strew clean straw
round her hindquarters, kneel
on either side, rub their hands warm
and nod, wordlessly,
across this county of her haunches.

One man cannot know
the other lost his first real job
bagging groceries at fourteen
for stealing a razor and blades.

One cannot know
his accomplice drowned
a litter of kittens when he was ten
to see how animals die.

Between them in the dim,
hay-dung chapel of this barn,
this cow will die in pain
if not relieved of her burden.

The veterinarian's needle penetrates
the bony ridge of her spine
and, vertebrae by vertebrae, inches
upwards from her tail.

Places a broad hand firmly
on the white expanse of swollen belly;
the scalpel in his other hand unzips her hide.
Hired man holds the furred edges apart
with his hands, and his companion
deftly draws his blade again and again
across the fine grain of her uterus,
its translucent tissues
peel themselves away, one by one.

At last, there is the womb.
Unborn calf in its hot,
aromatic pool. Warmth mists
the wrists of the hired man,
fogs his companion's glasses
as he lifts the bony form from its wet bed
and hands it glazed into the arms
of his assistant, who has taken down
a worn coat from a hook.

While the cow turns her head,
rolling her eyes white to see,
veterinarian clears the little one's
nose and mouth with his hands,
wraps the newborn in its borrowed coat
and lays it by the mother.

It would be easy to forget
how they removed the afterbirth
and sopped the fluids
from the cavity. To ignore
where they cast it aside for burial,
fixed instead upon the way
the two men kneel, as if humility
were an instinct and prerequisite.

Having no water except the freezing
well-stream in the tank outside,
they cleanse their hands
with antiseptic cream.

Then, while one holds together
the two halves of each peeled layer,
the other sews each pair of tissues
with a running stitch of stiff black threads
until the cavity and hide
are bound and closed again.

They stand and wipe their hands
on pocket handkerchiefs,
release the cow from tether
to rise when she can.
Nod and leave the darkened barn.

They have turned away already
to the separate courses
of their private histories and lives.

It will not occur to either man for years
that in the course of things
this calf was slaughtered for the table;
the cow dead, bitten by a snake.

Both men's marriages also gone,
divorce or loss, and both,
with small victories and large regrets,
quite possibly alive somewhere.

Dakota 1969

*If you want to write a song about the human race
...write a song about the moon.* Paul Simon

Call it a lace curtain or a veil. Call it
a tent of hyperbole or moonlight dissolving
in the kitchen. Call it a way home.

In the garden of wives there are sometimes
lovers, if not for long. Larking on horseback
among the prickly pear as if life is a Western
and they have the world on a string.

We are listening to the first moon landing
on transistor radio by candlelight, because
on earth's back forty the power has gone out.

Cattle are lowing in Auntie's corral:
season of separation, of call and response.

I wonder if the astronauts are singing
hallelujah in solitary whispers under their breaths.
Acoustics in helmets are terrible, they say.
No crowd noise in that earth-lighted stadium.

Last week a prairie fire lit up the bedroom
window like a furnace door and left a thousand
acres of pasture around the new missile silo
scorched, barren as the moon we once imagined.

I did not spark that sweeping conflagration
but memory has kept it burning.

After Courbet, Stars

"Deer in the Forest," Gustave Courbet 1868
Minneapolis Museum of Art

The doe has suckled the bitter cherry
and tonight the center of the world
is this hotel room beside a parking lot
where light from a Pabst sign in a tavern window
next door enlivens twinkling nebula and stars
on the ceiling above the bed.

As the stars are unreal, I will imagine
a twisting shadow among them as the Snake Nebula
observed in 1972 from a hotel bed in Keokuk

the unreal light years it has taken
for them to appear above me once again
negotiating transits like the paranoid man
in his football helmet, clutching a cricket bat
as he passes the tall Renwick Gallery steps
illuminated by light falling from its doorway
in 1977 where I am a momentary shadow.

Come morning with luck I will arise, ghostly
as the moon and its lover Venus
above the horizon of an 18-wheeler outside
and my waiting Volvo with its tumultuous miles

the road out there like shock waves
across the dawn, the distant highways
between galaxies I will call Dakota or Delaware.

Another backroads tour to save
school children who will never leave home
from an hour of Geography, to immerse
them in delicious words and dangerous possibilities

wondering if tomorrow night I may be
baptized if not born again in the arms
of the one unmarried teacher or sloe-eyed, unhappy
wife who believes a stranger may be a savior
or a passing comet, sworn for one night to shed
her burden, in the guise of saving his soul for poetry

or determined to leave him hurting
as I am now, lying under a static sky,
hurting in the place where poetry begins.

Tale of the Wise Men

An owl is watching the house.
Wherever there are owls, it is bad news
for someone. Black Elk saw

that if the old stories could survive,
he would have to trust white poets
to hear them. We can read what
Neihardt heard the old man's daughter
say her father said in that game of telephone.

Maybe it had something to do
with the gray clapboard exoskeletons
of houses, rising from burnt weeds
along the ridges, hills rising snowy
behind them. The gray people
beginning to arrive, to darken doorways
and stand unmoving at the windows.

We have not forgotten how crow
lost his voice. We do not use the word
"paltry" for what he brings to the manger.

Listen! There is saffron on the poet's bow.

Bane

I thought I had another year to kiss
the Doll's Eye Bane and call
the Saw-whet Owl out of the dark.

I had it from Gerald Stern, who taught me
how to be a Jew and not those know-it-alls
down at the Campus Snack, calling out
"Nurse" when they wanted beer
and hoo-hooing after her thunder thighs.

I thought I had another year to sow
a batch of slippery newbies in the pond,
to watch the mink slip under the ice
and harvest a crop of golden carp
on a sighing day in sweet October.

I had it from Lame Deer who showed me
how to be an Indian with his fable about
the Great Spirit and the Chicken,
though there was the question of Grandmother
in her doeskin wedding dress and quill beads.

And how I learned to talk again after years
of building haystacks by the creek, one line
of a poem cut into the grease and chaff
of the gearshift housing, and arriving over
and over with clenched teeth and only that to say.

I thought I had another year to kiss
the Doll's Eye Bane and call my cousins,
the Saw-whet and the Barred and the Great Horned Owl
out of the dark and, for those few minutes
of coded conversation, not be afraid.

Whether or No

What do you do if her old bay gelding
gets out and is struck by a train?

You remember it. That's what you do.

The first time I saw her Aunt Z
she was trying to die, a great sack
in a hospital bed, forehead creased
with the effort. The machine insisting
hup-breath, hup-breath, whether or no

the worried, troubled sack of her.
Nobody would stop it or make it stop.

Hup-breath. Hup-breath. Hup-breath.
Not a word could she say.

What if at long last they call on
the old poet himself to sing a beloved
favorite and he has forgotten the words?

What he does recall—the horse
and the midnight train, old woman,
the voice of the machine.

Also to take up his blackthorn stick
and take care not to fall into the fire.

Every Slow Thing

Reverie

She conjured a horse
that could walk on water.
Called it Ship. Mounted up
to ride over galloping waves.

She conjured a pack of wolves
that swore like collapsed Catholics.
Called them Vengeance.
They chased the villains into the river.

She conjured a brown cow
that had lost its calf. Called itself Charity.
When beggars came,
let down its milk to feed them.

She conjured a cockatoo,
snow white but for amber eyes.
Spoke in tongues with a raven's
deep chuckle. Its name was Paradox.

She conjured big cats, all named Al,
who took turns reciting
the Periodic Table, calling out names
like poor children in school.

She conjured at last great mountain sheep,
who turned themselves into ghosts
of her ancestors. She followed them
into the clouds and vanished.

Love in Time of Isolation

As if to a porchlight on a dark street
or familiar voice out of my sleep…
invitation dear as remembrance—shadow, swell, declivity
irresistible in any guise or shade of skin.

Those were the gifts I longed for and desired
and would abandon home or forfeit any peace to follow down.
Creating poetry by the flocking of words, the way
our forebears created myth by saying it and saying it again.

The old poet, Chameleon, becomes whatever comes into his yard.
Today a fox, riding an Appaloosa in the direction of the Soak
maybe in search of purple everlastings…riding…
Riding a horse named Awe through a pall of speechlessness
and absence.

Today cleanliness is next to godliness. We wash our hands.
In olden time we washed each other's feet for a religion.

As it was after the Battle of Mmaggèd, I climbed
the pulpit in the rustic church at Kent's Corner,
easier to climb up than climb down. Why did I always
find myself stranded—on a rooftop painting a steeple,
12 thousand feet up Mt. Evans and falling toward cascading lakes

giddy and overcome by a somnambulist from the orchestra, up
so many stairs too few nights above a country store
and wanting nothing more, nailing slippery slates
on her roof in pouring rain. Was it love or acrophobia?

Think of the way the violins in a requiem behave
and misbehave…that premonition.
Do not listen for the rattle of the calabash, they say.

Rules of Empire

A blind white dog stands shag deep in snow.
This back yard could be Bhutan, a woman
in plaid pajamas nearby milking a yak,
staring into the distance past a patch of grass
that might be Burma, where the horizon
is jagged with mountain tops of an island
country rife with birdsongs and trouble.

How far beyond to Java, where sleepers
of Bogar may be awakened by thunder
almost any night of the year.

There is jackfruit in Ceylon and mangoes.
A soldier rides a purring motorcycle in pure dark
toward a churchyard where a halo of light
encircles a tiny granite stone. A native girl
steps from the sidecar, mist on her face
and bare shoulders like a frisson of expectation.

These images, bitter and sweet, tug at the hem
of the reader's thoughts as he stands at the window,
facing the Bhutan of his morning. Thinking
yet of Ceylon where a priest and an astrologer
scratch their heads over a conundrum.

Not the same to them both, he thinks,
for the sin troubling the penitent seems wondrous
as yak milk to the lover, relishing what might ensue.
This disparity is surely a sort of miracle,
as only one of them is afraid of shadows.

Come morning, babies will hang in sacks of muslin
from the branches of trees, milk on their lips, asleep
while their mothers pick tea nearby.

The white dog will whine at the cold of Bhutan
and the woman in pajamas will pick him up
to go back inside their hut beyond the snow

and leave the reader with the matter of Ceylon
and its wonders, where the Governor has just left
his mistress, a dancing girl of a caste whose women
must go bare-breasted by rule of the Empire.

Ganz Andere

Full moon and the clouds cartwheeling.
How the world changes.
I'm 63 today
and watching brown bats come out,
my only aches from splitting wood with a maul.

I was moving plants when a large green frog
leaped over my shovel and larruped off to the pond
to spend the day impersonating rainwater.

At evening a shadow, big and round,
a bushel basket by the corner of the house
unfolded as I turned the key in the lock—shoulders,
legs and tail—and crept away.

Why must he carry his mother on his back?

Wasn't I exiled at an early age
by mystery—deep woods at nightfall,
black among the ostrich ferns,
lurking in stench under the outhouse,
secret back stair to the choir loft, wholly dark.

I've come home far from those
beliefs and fears.
I am the dog of uncertain parentage.
I am the dog who barks all night,
afraid of silence.

What will become of us?
Intrusions of the sacred everywhere.
Messages inside the bark of birches
are not prayers.

I heard him whistle.
The owls, they never heard of him.

"Without Fear of Wind or Vertigo"

—Italo Calvino, *If on a winter night a traveler*

Somnificence.
Naptime with mourning dove.

Gyre. I rise spinning like the poor
on bald tyres. (No snow in August.)

All fall down.
Circle for drop the handkerchief agus
run. Why this feeling of ascension,
This gimble in the wabe.

Grabe any old noise to stay put
(playing for keeps).

Four dayse and knights in hospital
(he fell off his horse) what they will say.
"Pour man, poor olde fellow he was."
Adrift. Purloined.

Outside my window in the world
of weeping willows the small birds hide
and squirrels who don't want to chase.

At the very top, buffeted by wind,
exposed but cowering and small,
one chaste—a wilding on a rocking horse
to and fro, maybe squirrel risking
pathetic fallacy. Wild-eyed, afraid. There
must be something between holding on
for dear life and the pursuit of happiness.

I once met an artist who drew auras
of poets and dancers she met. Just hands.
No trick, no guru—ink pen, infra-red film.

Storm outside, willows gambol and prance
like the end is at hand. Emerald female
hummingbird zips from scarlet pimpernel
to the hilt of a thrashing green willow whip.
Fearless bareback rider, that Sally.

Ruby-throated males ride the pendulum.
Females ride the wind.

White Porch

Vixen lopes across the yard,
lithe, her spring coat melted caramel
and white. Pauses

just beyond the scrim of willows
yellow in morning light to wait
for her dashing, distractible mate

nosing the margin of the woods,
reading the breeze that stirs new poplar leaves
to whispers, lifts traces of cedar bark, squirrel scat,

a calico cat, hiding in plain sight in a dappled pool
of sun, syncopated pats of a blue butterfly's
feet, probing the honeysuckle and hornbeam,

lingering screed of estrus where yesterday
a burly carpenter climbed in among the scrub
and lady ferns and skunk cabbage

and later emerged, pulling up her drawers,
whiz of hummingbird at the open mouths
of pink coral bells, this now this.

Aura of the woman who has stepped out
onto the white porch across the way that rides
the stillness like a lifeboat on a green wave;
white nightgown moth-like as she bares
her arms above her tousled head

and sighs away sleep. Catbird, cardinal,
least flycatcher silent, bees on the dogtooth
violets, turtle's nest and hidden eggs
vouchsafed to the mulch.

Fox hears the low whine in vixen's throat,
strikes a pose among the hosta: regal brush,
looks as if he might make a life, or
at least a quiet chapter of such things.

Witness

He lived in the valley of five winds
across the street from a somnambulist
of the orchestra, where the twins,
men of a certain age, came and went past
at a certain time each day,
walking the gantlet of his gaze.

Perhaps they were lords of a manor
in another part of town.
Perhaps they were, like himself, nobodies,
their drab, once-black trousers
and white shirts interchangeable

except for their names, maybe stitched
onto their pockets, also interchangeable.

He tried to imagine their inheritance, lords
or nobodies—one the tune, the other
the book—and the first had received the gift
of dreams. Two aspects of a first principle.

Was he always the same who strode first,
lines of a poem by Pope in his head,
like Alan Rickman as King Louis XIV,
believing he "has grown too old for jokes"

and who followed, laconically, seeing crows
on a wire as the opening chord of a song,
humming truncated phrases of "Here's
That Rainy Day" a dozen paces behind?

And where do they go? To Red's, where
the wild one, Tess, pours a generous jar?

Or the P.O., expecting or hoping
a letter and from whom?

Were they once in love with the same
raven-haired beauty, who could not
make up her mind? Or was that himself and she
who taught him as Par Lagervist wrote:
that "meaninglessness, too, is divine."

Olly Olly Oxen Free

Alice awoke from a dream of Hide-and-Seek,
where she was hiding, blind and naked
in a place she knew, far from the house,
down the skipping orchard lane
where no one would find her. She knew

how she could run away to a remote
and secret house from long ago,
moon-faced owl for a companion,
hesitating wooden creak of stable door, ajar
to view the coming dark, also hesitating.
The way she knew between dissolving shapes
of pear and apple trees. Their scented blossoms.

Soft saddle blanket on a bale of hay.
If only she had a horse, at least a hairbrush.
A brother who could teach her boy things.
She could teach him how to put on lipstick,
crawl behind the bed and hold your breath
to kiss. Or put on music like her mother.
Hold your arms out—one-two-three—and dance.

Smell can tell who comes—stale cigarette
and sweat is uncle. Grandfather, his pipe tobacco
and scotch. West is wind from the river,
crayfish smell and mud. East is faint chlorine
from a neighbor's swimming pool. Here
is fox urine of the flower bed outside the door.
Leather, horse and pigeon poop inside.

Shiver of ginkgo leaves. Whisper of rain.
Others talk as if she is not there. As if she
didn't know what shade of girl her skin could be.
A hairbrush would be nice. She has nice hair.

What if no one had called her in?

Omenclature

What if soul is the fairy ping
inside a spent light bulb?

In the lagoon of a forest bromeliad
a frog so small it could not
find itself in the class picture.

How were we children to know
the Ark of the Covenant
was not a boat?

Don't give up on the ridiculous.

The frieze at the cathedral door:
lambs and bunnies at the bottom
made the children smile.

Ogres and fornicating humans
caused adults to swallow hard
and duck inside.

Sleep like lake water,
lapping but won't come over me.
Staring into the dark, I am
shadow-boxing with my past selves.

So many kinds of fool.

On the Death of a Small Child

Zum erstaunen bin ich da. Goethe*

Some will ask
what was he doing here at all?

One house full of sleeping,
another of grief.
My part, to rise again and again,
keeping the chimney warm.

One day the stories the children
tell will be astonishing.
How woods in new snow are luminous.
How recent the Ice Age seemed
this morning.

The earliest elephant
was the size of a pig.
Improbable wooly mammoth
would wander the world again,
stuffing itself with its snout,
grinding up grasses with molars
the size of curbstones.

Why didn't the awful troll
under the bridge have a name?
And when did the flying dinosaurs
learn to sing?

When there were tall women
in the house, he chewed their hair.
When there was milk,
he was the nearest mouth.

When the meteor struck,
it was a darkening event
that changed the world.

I am here to wonder.

Circus

Beauty with inner implications...
is beauty that makes an artist of the viewer.
—Soetsu Yanagi

That was a storied summer.
Hawks were haggard
and the girls untamed.

I heard them before I saw them.
Round the bend of a hoof-worn lane,
two women, nut-brown and naked
to the waist, wielding axes
in dazzling syncopation.

We do not want some stories to end
because the pause that ensues
will be endless.

We want the harrier hawk
to keep circling the rabbit forever.

We want there to be a next birth
when a child has died,
a next wife, next lover, next finch
for the cage left empty,
next pup in the house out back
with the wrong name over the door.

But a new story will not end that silence.

These trees, those women,
my father and mother,
perhaps even their disappointments,
their regrets, will be reborn
—as paths in the garden,
as beardtongue and stonecrop by the path,
as blue butterflies or clouds of smoke.

Self-Portrait with Cat

As if a fool might give
a wise account of himself,
whose past is a patchwork
of regrets and non sequiturs

to whom every embrace was a gift
and every kiss a leaving.

There is no cat on the big red chair.

It is true, I have a mouth
for Irish whiskey and stomach
for the porridge of knowledge.
A heart for song and a wild eye for beauty

and desire, like the old anger, simmers still.

A white cat would be portentous.

Mother and father dead,
orphaned by my children,
family lore about some class of Indian,
the one thing certain of my heritage
is that I'm neither fish nor fowl.

And no longer waiting to be famous.

An old cat with tufted ears seems right,
sleepy there against a pillow, sanguine.

There is my farmer neighbor, Boone,
alighting from the school bus, face and hands
bloodied, as if a barn cat had attacked him
for sitting on its tail at tea.

He has been trying a new approach
to the high jump called the forward roll
over barbed-wire fences in the field.

What of a barn cat out of the feral Marn,
who fled forlorn alleys of London in a grim century?

Fifty years ago I was awakened quaking
from fitful sleep in a stone *pension*
across the street from the church
of St. Sebastian in Salzburg
by the soul-sundering *wrong* and again
wrong of a massive bell that began the clang
and chime of bells across the entire city,
their Matins calls.

There hangs the haunting, life-sized,
painted wooden Madonna,
ten-inch hilt of a dagger protruding
from the top of one bleeding breast
in company of the agonizing Christ
with his mocking crown of thorns.

Would that the cat were Ozymandias,
King of Cats in his morning coat and cravat.

What did I write then I cannot now
—that long-ago singing to that long-ago girl
and who was she to ignite my song?

Come back now: the hillside, the copse
of trees, the summer rain
and herself, eager as I was and almost
as young—loving what we did and didn't do

until she got up and ran, taking her name
with her. What difference would it make
if this were true? Such love
needs neither names nor bed,
a holly bush to hang a garment on will do.

Loss is the bed we learned to lie upon.
Remember the pebbles soft as kisses
against your windows, the stones
hard as desire unbridled at your door.

I've seen my words in print and paint,
in hammered copper, cut into steel,
yet recall them not at all. They've gone
like the cat who might have been.

Elegy

Neither in the garden, nor on a bench by the door.
—Louis de Bernieres, *Notwithstanding*

Where should I look for the man I was?
Absent father. Wayward son.

In baptistry waters, neither saved
nor drowned.

At the elbow of a Lakota child,
pencil gripped hard, hunched over
a gaggle of wild words on a page.

At the shoulder of a pianist, eyes closed
to the minor chords that insinuate opening
phrases of "Every Time We Say Goodbye."

Singing a cappella sans tipsy organist
from a Choteau choir loft, "Lo, how a rose
ere blooming," at Christmas mass.

At the hospital bedside of my righteous brother
in his darkest hour, recalling the name
of a Dutch prostitute he encountered in innocence
on the night ferry from Dover to Calais.
She had asked if he had a light.

In Osnabrück, Glasthule, in Paris, or looking down
on the bear pits of Bern. In Salzburg among
the Mozart graves. Among fishmongers of Marseille.
In Dingle or Dublin or remote Donegal.

With apostles of the astronomical clock in Prague.
MacLellan's Castle ruin and kirk in Kirkcudbright.
Channeling Vermeer on canals in Delft. Halls
of the Met. Mother, father, two brothers all dead
and others sick and I could do nothing about it.

And everywhere but here, a stranger.

Anthropology

Was it 40,000 years ago or only forty
when we learned to tilt our heads
so our noses would not keep our lips
from touching? But anyway before

that game of bobbing for apples floating
in a tub and our foreheads touched
or bumped, really, which was how
the thought of love got into my head.

And I still have the bony forehead welt,
like a sensor, sore if I press on it,
though that may have been
the corner of a bookshelf where I kept
my favorites—Eliot and Alcosser and Bly

—and hid the key to a diary with names
to help recall eye color and the shapes of lips
up close, droplets of water on the tips
of eyelashes and noses. Or tears, thanks be.

Nocturne No. 2 in E Flat Major

Listening to Chopin while dusting
a treasured clay pot on my shelf, round
as a cantaloupe. On its shoulder, a subtle sheen
where ash, rising like smoke in the heat
of a wood fire at the base of the kiln

to swirl for a night and a day
among the naked rows of jars and pots,
settled weightlessly at last

here where my duster of sheep's wool
busses away ephemera, as it seems, of time
from a whorl like the areola of a lover's breast
amid umber constellations that were but clouds
of gasses we believe we might have touched
in a distant galaxy and time.

And here, the delicate lip defines
an open mouth, too small for any
but an infant's hand to probe inside
where the potter (ear and heart to the thrum
of his wheel) augured the slip,
within and without, a membrane apart,
as the clay took shape.

We may imagine whatever we like
in that black nothingness—a small spider
in a brown fedora, smoking a cheroot.
Minding a tiny packet of shadows
he will unfold if you ask. You may be sorry.

We may also imagine the artist's handmaid
at work with brush and broom, modest
in her chambray shirt, moving with easy grace
among the jars and pots, milk jugs, pitchers
and giant vases of a studio that smells
of earth and cloves and stale tobacco.

Notice how the music of the piano lingers
like a slow rain on a stranger's roof.

Nude in a Cathedral Window

Next door, the grand barn window
of a stained-glass studio. A figure lies
on the broad sill inside, skin like terracotta.

Art students wipe charcoal dust
from their hands and abandon their easels.

In the geometry of summer lassitude
an ensemble of musicians surrounds her,
improvising harmonics and hues
that resonate among her shadows and swells.

Refractions of sunlight cast a border
of fish round her window like prayer flags.
The air perfumed with the scent
of laneway Century trees.

Later they may take off their shoes
and approach her unafraid.

Over in Christ Church the choir singers
have come to practice in the nave;
the Quality of Mercy soars into the arches.

The psychoanalyst in her salon
murmurs something about iconography
and crosses her legs.

Who is the man outside the window
on whom the girl reclining smiles?

This is the mad monk's inhabited letter
in the Third Book of Djinn,
where the poet interprets the dream.

Every Slow Thing

Awoke, alone
in a hotel room, a word
in my mouth. *Isthmus.*

There is beauty
in every slow thing.

Tonight O'Hare Airport
a woman materializes
among the teeming crowd.

How light clings to her shift,
shaping her as mountain slopes
and glades of light and shade.

Isthmus, I say to no one
as if…*isthmus* she moves
a languid symmetry.
As if translucent,
a liquefaction of shadow and light.

Call her *Isthmus.* Or *Jeroboam.*
I say it in a whisper: *Jeroboam.*

Chicago, I say to myself. *Rococo.*
The tumult has fallen away.
Pulse of the room decrescendo.

And she approaches like a…
tidal shift, a mirage at sea perhaps.
What errand? What insouciance.

Hello, I mean to say.
Enchanté. But nothing *entre nous.*

Asp of Jerusalem

Woad.
Also cabbage blue.
Fierce, the Picts of old
were the cabbage men.

It was after berry-picking
somewhere Illinois.
A stranger. Invited to join
naked swimmers in a pond.

They were not beautiful.
They were young.

Like being in a play in which
the poet Pablo Neruda plays himself.
So far from home and no regrets.

In the aspens yellow-bellied sapsuckers
laughed themselves blue.

As Beauty Does

Who would not love
the painter's model, her mouth
on canvas bleeding from a kiss.

The cat's paw birthmark
on bold Samantha's thigh made famous
by the coming in of mini-skirts.

A sleepwalker
naked about the neighborhood
but for morning fog.

Or Nurse Pushkin,
eyelids fluttering, asleep beside me
just before her apartment fire.

I've known beauty and know beauty still.

Kiss the Lion

—Looking Glass Theatre, Chicago

Houselights come up
we clatter through the lobby
buoyant, elated   wildness clinging to us
like wool and whimsy and the crackle of laughter.

Our minds clutch remnants we liked best
to recall over whiskey or when we sit alone.
How she how they, the fireplace mirror an illusion
how a ring a rope can mime a rabbit hole
the giant queen her black mustache
the Hare a-scamper down a row of chairs

and how in a golden age of skin
after a swim an actress knelt
beside the mirror of a neighbor's pool
a glimpse   a pause   the ladder of her hem
and I a useless pronoun   wanton
gems of water on her secret hair.

Those pebbles later at her window so
ca-co-pho-nous   she will she won't
the white knight on a silver bicycle will
crash and clattering to bits   a metaphor
but then return astride his wheel a plethora
of dear mistakes much like our own
regrets gathered will-he nil-he in his arms.

A song next door, a peacock's cry or else
the cat in pain reminds us
of a laughing moon   the ladder of her hem

and when she ate the rose   was it a fake
a ladder to the balcony   and did we
did he really fall?

Daydream 20 years and more the Hatter mad,
the whiskey good again, that play, the pool
o puss, o purse o sighing hills.
Wasn't there a lion?

Robyn of the Snows

Here is a Hubble photograph
of the Snowflake Cluster, 900 light years
beyond Orion and here

is a woman who invited me a very long
time ago to accompany her to see
nesting eagles on a remote mountain side
in eastern Wyoming.

It had begun to snow. We would sit
perfectly still and the eagles
would rise, she said; would materialize
before our eyes as earlier, seated
on a low sofa in her apartment

within easy arms' reach, our favorite
versions of our lives rose to become
almost palpable between us
so we could love them or love instead
what we wanted to believe about each other.

So we were silent on the mountain,
our whole attention a unison
of expectation and the snow
fell upon our shoulders and rose there
until we could feel its weight, our
selves vanishing even as when

we open our eyes in the dark
we may believe ourselves invisible.
The eagles if they were inside
the falling snow did not rise. And
as darkness came on, the slope

that had consumed our long attention
faded to white silence. I do not
recall our rising or our going. It seems
almost as far away as this star cluster
and as immaterial now, whether

we may have heard cries or wingbeats,
or if we were overjoyed then or afraid.

Night-walking

Whatever you would put in you would take out,
leaving only the residue of taste.
—French chef Andre Soltner on Sauce Béarnaise

The woman in my dream led night-walking
and spoke in tongues.
Said the caliph's assassins were turned into owls.

Said the Pelican Nebula is composed of ink,
enough to write until the end of time.
Said a dust pillar at the rim of Carina Nebula
resembles a man fleeing a burning house.

Said morning's children would awake
to clouds of curds and whey.
And the knowledge that our Sun
is just a garden-variety star.

And I woke to the white eyes of shadowy deer
bedded down on snow at the edge of the woods
and saw they were ghosts of ourselves asleep
in the moon-moored house.

Standing barefoot at the window
I heard the confessions of owls and other ghosts:
hum of trucks on the distant wire of the highway,
sighs of a midnight train racing its shadow on the river.

Things to Say Underwater

When crows roost, the day is over.
What is a suitable prayer?
Is one a suitable number?

Married five times, the bartender
said old man made a bridge of cobwebs.
And her saying made it so.

It must also be said, she married for love
every time. No wonder,
yet a pity, she never married me.

Loving is a craft
that demands excess
and rewards restraint.
I did not marry her again and again.

The Hermit Speaks to His Dogs

Time was, I had some badges
and some wives, some spice-skinned
women on satin sheets,
their perfumed soaps, their musky oils.

Courted in white silk
and white linen shoes. My car,
pearl gray, the inside redolent
of leather and plums.

There were barefoot cellists
and Chopin nocturnes
in country gardens I helped to make.
Bach string quartets on shady canals.

Girls were a tangle of limbs
in the baths. You dogs—Toulouse,
Goethe, Trotsky and Bosch—
your tongues would never tire of their salt.

I was the hunter and I was the prey.

A pipe for me, and for you, a bowl.
I braided those Croatian ties
round your necks. A Lebanese girl
made this quilt for our bed.

I know you listen
when I talk to dear ghosts
like Em, who once in Montana
sleep-walked naked to my door.

This bundle of letters, I keep
by my pillow. Fervent words
in flowery hands. Now

tobacco gone; our fire gone out.
Lie heavy and do not
whimper or whine. Remember
how I slept with Maggs in her fever.

The Poet, Old School

He imagined words as silhouettes
of former creatures—nouns as animals
shorn of fur and leather, verbs as birds
adorned in wings and feathers. So

he believed, and no wonder,
they could be made to sing and sin,
to romp and roar.

If we could learn to listen,
they become themselves, for instance,
the flautist Hermit Thrush on the cliff
at Carraig Binn, a Laughing Thrush
chortling at a sidewalk table in Hawaii.

The snake in Eden's Garden,
its insouciance, its cool sanguinity.

Old Man Feet

No one cares where the broom was born.
Or the broom-maker who first bound
a fistful of straw to sweep ash from the hearth
and sand from the threshold.

Or whether Grandfather's draft horses
Dolly and Babe were buried or reduced
to upholstery, whips, and glue.

No one cares for old man feet.
Topography of knobs and veins
begun to warp. Dolly and Babe,
bound to pull in different directions.

One darker, one pale. One foolish,
one cautious. One inclined to good;
the other always listing.

How light they were: right first,
left trailing over hurdles on the cinder track;
left thrust, right lift in flight
over chains and country fences.

Uncertain now which suffered the cut
while wading naked in the creek, blood
vivid, faint scar in the bark of the sole.
Both, still afraid of the dark.

Translucent skin, nails like hooves.
Restless during naps, dogs
dreaming the chase, recalling miles
of our traveling days—dim alleys,
side doors, sweet attic rooms.

Left one cramps while making love.
Right one going first down stairs
the morning after.

Sufficient unto the Day

Countless weeks, countless months
of gestation. After seeds
fell out of the sky, after the faceless
planes went home and flowers rose

out of Hiroshima and Nagasaki

poison ivy along foreign borders
land mines, garden variety
nuisance wars

this deflowering of America.

This time our planes
lodged in the tuning forks of tall
buildings.

This time we could hear
the roar, the downward wind
the clamor clamor clamor

nearby in the neighborhoods
we thought we heard
singing of metal, choiring stairs,

what a madrigal of collapse.

What of the figure falling
from the burning tower?
If I keep this image,
if I keep repeating the question

will he or she if it was she
live forever?

Weights and Measures

In the New Year we imagine
the snow begins to sing.
Also the mud. We remember
the sadness caught in its throat.

There was war when I walked
to kindergarten, and I was afraid
of shadows as I went through the woods.
The little rug I had to borrow
at naptime had sadness in it.

How many times
have I slept through the birth
of the seventeen-year locusts?
How many lovers have slept beside me,
waiting to leave in the morning?

Because we are older now,
someone will ask us to lead the way.
We will try to recall a story
with a lesson in it.

For My Wife on Her Birthday

She goes to bed
as Sleeping Beauty
and wakes up
as all of the Seven Dwarfs

in some older rendition
where they are
seven orphans kidnapped,
escaped into hiding, or

errant knights
each with a different charm
or task, or coppiced
by a curse
in which there must
be horses, a glass coffin
blood on snow

or seven monks
in singlets, cutting firewood
while reciting esoteric
verses, saints

because there must be saints
blue with cold or radiant
with tongues of flame
who swear and foreswear
seven sins.

One who sells apples.
One who walks backward
with faggots in her arms,
speaking Irish.

One who recollects
dreams of fleeing soldiers,
of sisters a kitchen a stolen child.

One who remembers
everything
however trifling:

initials on a kerchief
laces on a boot
a bell on a bicycle

first lines
parting words
the smell of a man
what everyone said.

There Is a Saying in Swahili

There is a saying in Swahili
that might have greeted Mungo Park
when he first laid eyes on the Niger

and has since drifted in and out
of ordinary discourse, unpardonably
misquoted by preachers at the onset
of funeral eulogies, inexplicably
favored by motivational speakers
and overheard in halftime locker rooms.

It is not unlikely Lincoln struck it
from his notes before the speech
at Gettysburg or Appomattox
or that Ben Franklin paraphrased it
in Poor Richard's Almanac.

It was what, after the Battle of the Bulge,
Winston Churchill had meant to say.

And if someone said Obama had alluded
to it, speaking to the Navy Seals
who had Bin Laden in their sights,
or Tenzing Norgay muttered it to Hillary
as they looked across the summit
of Everest toward China and Tibet
we should not be surprised.

Poets from the great Lord Tennyson
to T.S. Eliot and Yeats have coveted
its measured sweetness and subtle tones.

It might have been the final words
of St. Catherine of Siena, Joan of Arc
or Giordano Bruno to the flames.

It might well have been etched
into a thousand granite stones.

Paleo Truleo

— after a photograph by Malcolm Kirk,
New Guinea, National Geographic July 1969

Clay man waits for ancestor to come.
Blue clay on his skin, flaking.
Waits a long time.

Clay jar a crude hive on his head.
Holes for breathing.
Whisk of magic leaves in his hand.

He is Quiet, awaiting the whisper
when old one comes.
To tell. To command. To sing.

Inside his mask
is the center of the world.
Where Silence is the heart's thunder.

He is practicing an uncertain word.
To still the hammer of his pulse
in the jar. To mend his stammer.

He awaits the invention of ink.
Singing to himself. No self.
Cry like a rainy day.

Ah, Now

Look at me, a drop of the best
and smoking an old briar pipe left me
by my father half-century ago

warm, cap to toe in old woolens, recalling
my old dog, the philosopher MacDuff,
my old Maine Coon cat Moshu
with his princely tail, gone rogue
to sleep in the woods in abandoned cars

and old time religion, good enough
for them all, my cousins and brothers,
for Grandma Winnie at the pump organ
in the little brown church in the vale.
My old Chevy car from before the war,
dear mother said it could run on fumes.

Look at me, lifting a toast to the flaming light
in the tops of beeches at sunset,
wood smoke curling from chimneys
in the hollow, geese bleating overhead,
migrating sparrows mobbing the lawn,
woodpeckers and finches and tits at the feeders

gorgeous wife giving me sly looks, you'd think
I was old what's-his-name
with the glasses and pen, the laurels and titles
and feathers in his cap,
the silver this and golden that, a home
and a passport, money, and three wishes
still unspent in my travel bag.

Nine Green Apples

Nine green apples and one red.
My life.

Think of the newborn.
He has no yesterday.

He thinks god is a breast,
that love is a fullness on the tongue,
the swollen lips…
This belief may persist for a lifetime.

Whom shall I ask for words
to console my spirit?

Here is an old song learned in childhood:
"Bye, baby bunting. Daddy's gone
a-hunting. To catch a little rabbit skin…"
What sort of lullaby for a vegetarian?

Will you mind if I hum
as I gather some lovage, some rhubarb,
some lemon thyme?

With so many apples
I cannot help singing.

The Palmist

Her children burn their prayers
so they will go out on the wind.

She says: Look at this circle
this line look at this hand.
See these loves these children
this one you have told no one.

Here you will die and here
get up again.
This means some power this
girdle round the pointing finger
some knowing.

These lines on the thumb's
fundament you had lives before.
These bracelets you live longer
and again.

Who judges the porcupine,
turning, slow as a teapot, in the road.

You will see your true love
in disguise, a stranger.
It is a game she plays,
changing her clothes, her name.

Prophecy

—Astronomers predict that the massive Andromeda
galaxy will overwhelm the Milky Way in 2.5 billion years.

It's a provocative rumor:
"Andromeda is coming."

What shall we non-believers
make of it then?

Some will envision
Andromeda
in her diaphanous blue shift,

descending a star-dusted stair
      with an aura of entitlement
            on the eve of her marriage.

Some, having witnessed the lurid reds
and tidal winds
of other galactic courtships
with their pinwheels, tops and exploding cigars,

look forward to a testicular collision
of gasses and swirling ovarian clouds,
angel choirs and sweet, unbridled howlings.

Think of a cosmic cathedral like Chartres,
the awesome rose window
an incandescent whirlpool
of visible sounds.

All the children at the Sunday School
are singing "Andy loves me, this I know."

Prophets in sandals will shield their eyes
and roar in outdoor voices:

She'll be driving six white horses when she comes!

While poets pipe in still, small voices:
"Heaven help us. The cat is out of the bag."

Before

Nobody has big ideas at noon.

There must be shadows.
Say, in the hour before
dawn's early light before

dogs begin to bark at shadows, before
wind picks up before
hemlocks and hornbeams and beeches
shake themselves awake, before

sanctity's color touches the yellow
apple tree planted when she died, before
wind alarms its leaves as it did
when it blew out the candles
and tangled our thin voices, before

baritones from the bell tower
of the Dom awaken cobblestones
under the hotel window and lovers
lie hearing each other breathing,

before cells reinvent the body and its
follicles and corpuscles
and the fictions of memory and self

before wizards stall the world's clocks
half a second before they
toll twelve on the last day of the year

before the specter strikes a bell
and twelve wooden apostles appear
chained to the millstone of history

before so many errors.

About the Author

Daniel Lusk is author of eight poetry collections and other books. His work is published widely in literary journals and anthologies, and his genre-bending essay, "Bomb" *(New Letters),* was awarded a Pushcart Prize. He has been Visiting Poet at Stranmillis University College of Queen's University Belfast, The Frost Place (Franconia, NH), and Juniata College (Huntingdon, PA), and a Writing Fellow at Yaddo and The MacDowell Colony. Well known for his poetry workshops and a former commentator on books for NPR, he is now a Senior Lecturer of English Emeritus at the University of Vermont. A native of the prairie Midwest, he lives in Vermont with his wife, Irish poet Angela Patten.

Poetry by Daniel Lusk

Every Slow Thing

The Shower Scene from Hamlet

The Vermeer Suite

KIN

Lake Studies: Meditations on Lake Champlain

The Inland Sea: Reflections (audiobook)

Kissing the Ground: New & Selected Poems

The Cow Wars